SCRAPBOOK SEQUENCES
VOLUME 8

Enter the Dragon: The Legacy of a Martial Arts Classic
50th Anniversary issue

Enter the Dragon, released in 1973, was a ground-breaking martial arts movie that had a profound impact on its worldwide audience. Directed by Robert Clouse, and starring Bruce Lee in his final completed film role, the movie was a cultural phenomenon that helped to popularize martial arts around the world.

At the time of its release, Enter the Dragon was considered a ground breaking film for several reasons. Firstly, it was one of the first movies to feature martial arts prominently, and it did so in a way that was both stylish and exciting. The movie's fight scenes were expertly choreographed and performed by the talented cast, including Bruce Lee, who was already a martial arts icon by this point in his career. The film's success helped to establish martial arts as a legitimate form of entertainment, paving the way for future movies and television shows in the genre.

Secondly, Enter the Dragon was one of the first movies to bring together international talent from both sides of the Pacific. The film was a co-production between Hong Kong's Golden Harvest studio and Warner Bros. Pictures, and it featured a diverse cast of actors from the US, Hong Kong, and other countries. This cross-cultural collaboration helped to broaden the appeal of the film and cemented its place in cinematic history.

Finally, Enter the Dragon was notable for its themes of honour, respect, and discipline. These themes were central to Bruce Lee's personal philosophy and were reflected in the movie's plot and characters. The film's message of self-improvement and self-mastery resonated with audiences around the world, inspiring countless individuals to take up martial arts and to strive for personal excellence in their own lives.

In the years since its release, Enter the Dragon has continued to have a significant impact on popular culture. The movie has been re-released and re-mastered multiple times, allowing new generations of viewers to experience its timeless appeal. It has inspired countless imitators and homages, from the Kill Bill movies to the video game series Mortal Kombat. Its iconic soundtrack, composed by Lalo Schifrin, has been sampled and referenced in numerous songs and other works of art.

As we approach the 50th anniversary of Enter the Dragon's release, it is clear that the film's legacy has only grown stronger over time. Its impact on the world of martial arts and popular culture is undeniable, and it continues to inspire and entertain audiences around the globe. The film's message of honour, respect, and discipline remains as relevant today as it was in 1973, and its influence can be seen in everything from the rise of mixed martial arts to the on-going popularity of kung fu movies. For fans of martial arts, cinema, and popular culture, Enter the Dragon will always be a classic that stands the test of time.

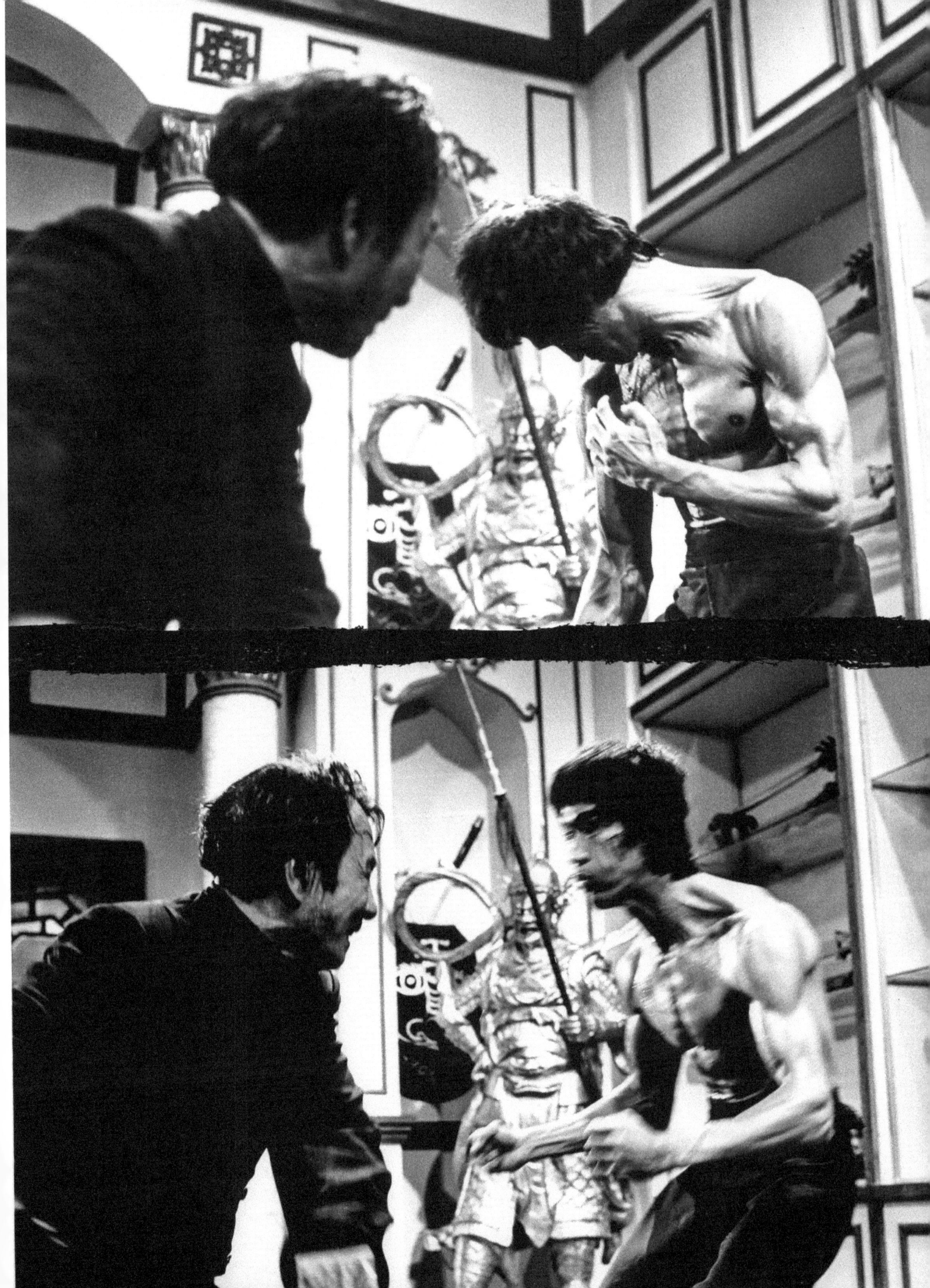

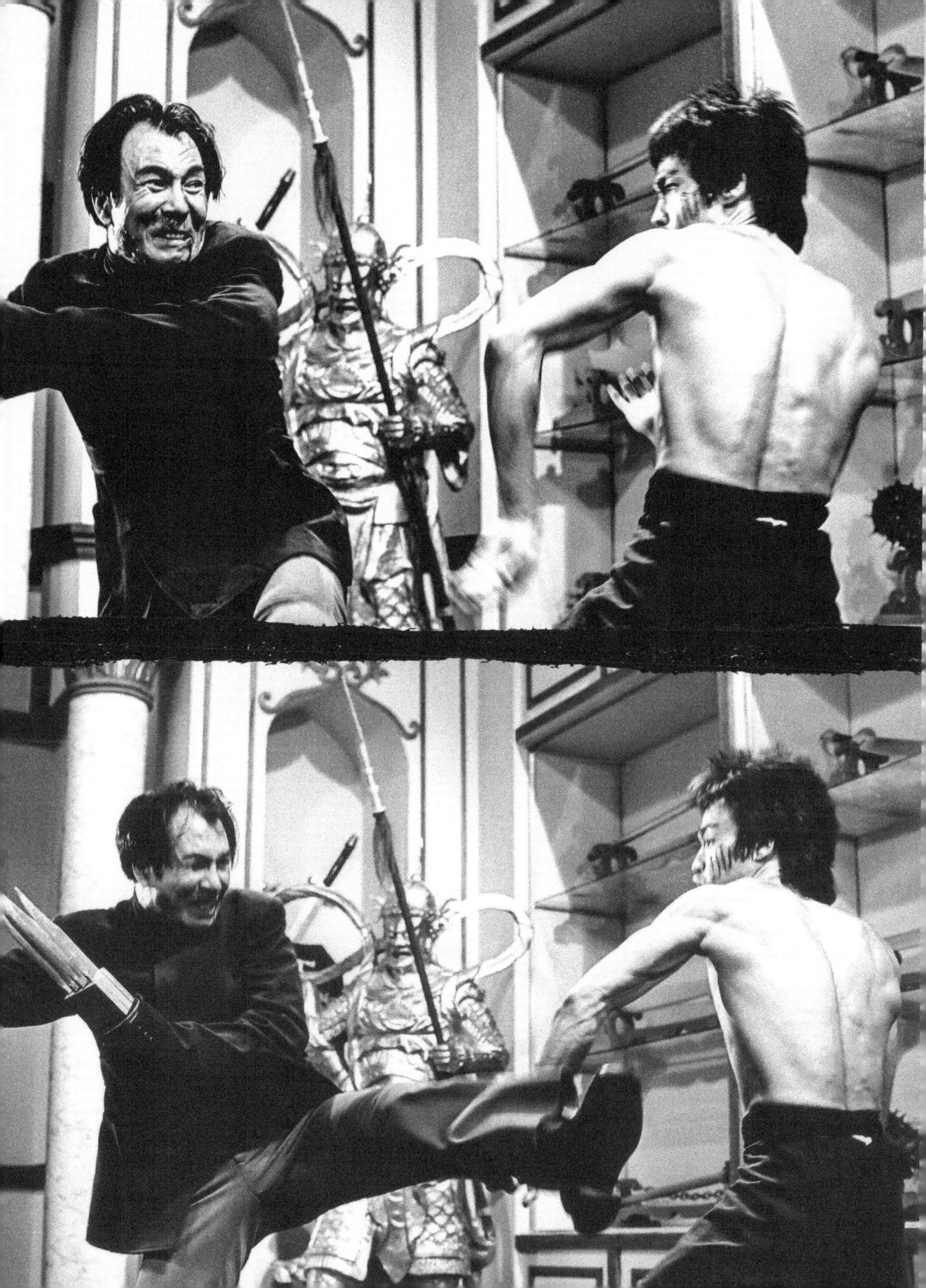

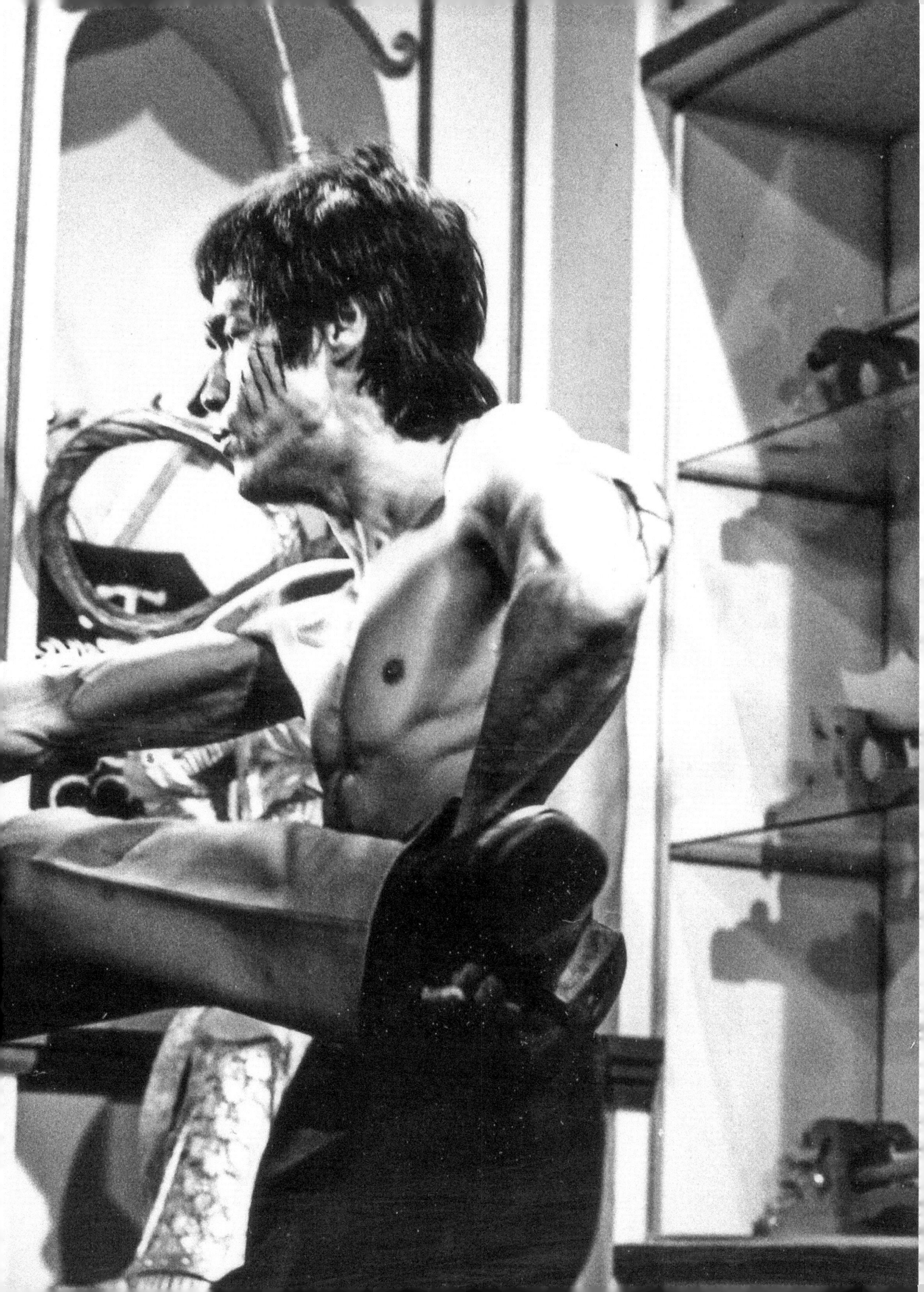

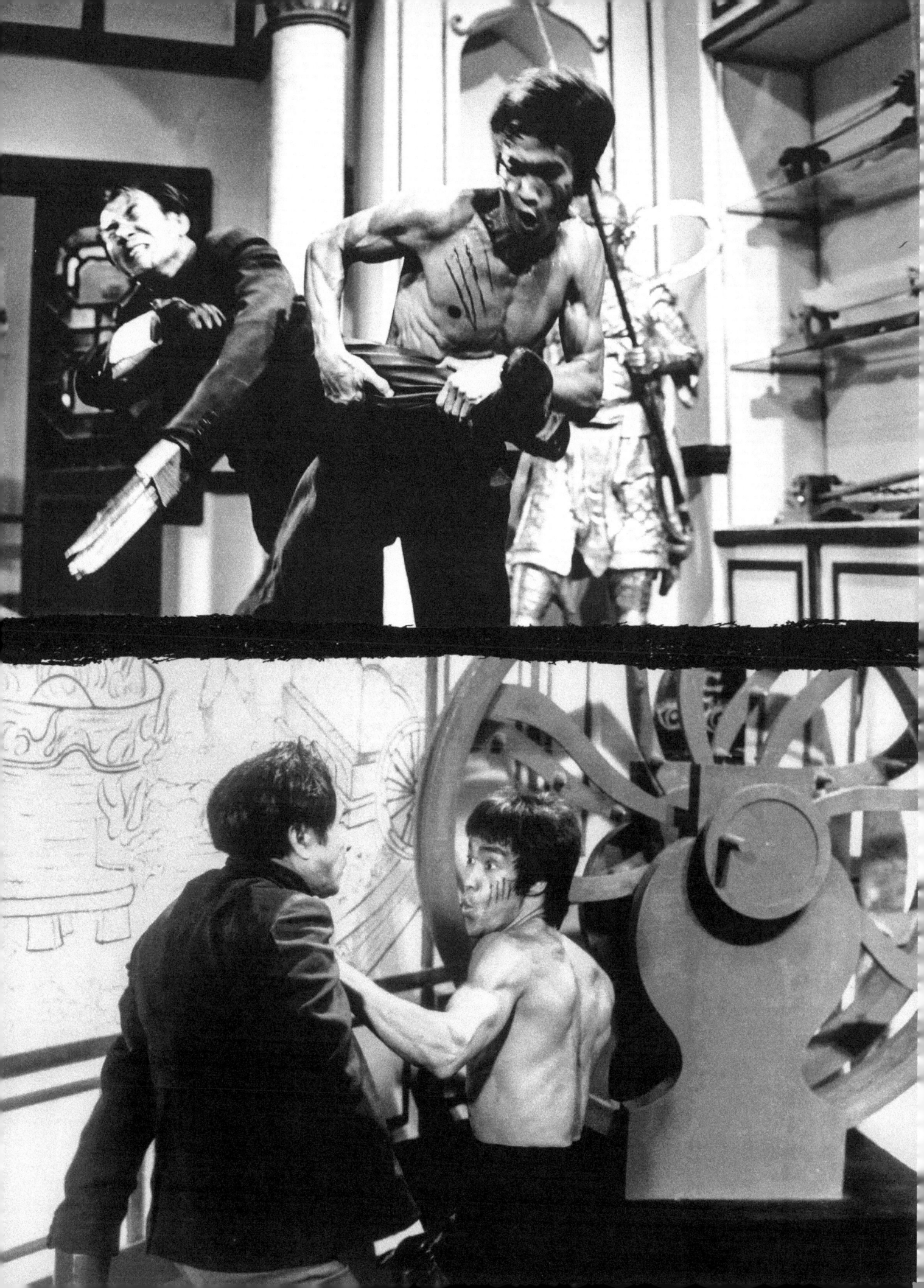

www.ingramcontent.com/pod-product-compliance
Lightning Source LLC
Chambersburg PA
CBHW042028100526
44587CB00029B/4331